The Typical Bitcoin

By; Wanda B. Roberts

Introduction

"Bitcoin has no proprietor, no power that can settle on its destiny. It is possessed by the group, its clients. What's more, it currently has a history of quite a while, enough for it to be a creature by its own doing. Simple presence is an insurance contract will remind legislatures that the last article the foundation had some control over, specifically, the money, is presently not their syndication. This gives us, the group, an insurance contract against an Orwellian future."

Chapter 1

A thorough and definitive investigation of Bitcoin and its place in money related history

At the point when a pseudonymous software engineer presented "another electronic money framework that is completely shared, with no confided in outsider" to a little web based mailing list in 2008, not many individuals focused. After a decade, and despite everything, this upstart independent decentralized programming offers a relentless and worldwide open hard cash option in contrast to current national banks. The Bitcoin Standard examines the verifiable setting to the ascent of Bitcoin, the monetary properties that have permitted it to develop rapidly, and its probable financial, political, and social ramifications.

While Bitcoin is a development of the computerized age, the issue it indicates to tackle is just about as old as human culture itself: moving worth across existence. Writer Saifedean Ammous takes the peruser on a drawing in venture through the historical backdrop of advances carrying out the roles of cash, from crude frameworks of exchanging limestones and shells, to metals, coins, the highest quality level, and present day government obligation. Investigating what gave these innovations their financial job, and how most lost it, gives the peruser a smart thought of what makes for sound cash, and makes way for a monetary conversation of its ramifications for individual and cultural future-direction, capital collection, exchange, harmony, culture, and workmanship. Compellingly,

Ammous shows that it is no fortuitous event that the loftiest accomplishments of mankind have come in social orders partaking in the advantages of sound financial systems, nor is it unintentional that money related breakdown has typically went with civilizational breakdown.

With this foundation set up, the book continues on to make sense of the activity of Bitcoin in a practical and natural manner. Bitcoin is a decentralized, conveyed piece of programming that changes over power and handling influence into unquestionably exact records, subsequently permitting its clients to use the Internet to carry out the customary roles of cash without depending on, or trust, any specialists or framework in the actual world. Bitcoin is subsequently best perceived as the main effectively carried out type of computerized cash and advanced hard cash. With a mechanized and entirely unsurprising financial strategy, and the capacity to perform last settlement of huge totals across the world in no time, Bitcoin's genuinely upper hand may very well be as a store of significant worth and organization for the last settlement of enormous payments—a computerized type of gold with an implicit settlement foundation.

Ammous' strong handle of the innovative potential outcomes as well as the verifiable real factors of financial development accommodates an intriguing investigation of the implications of deliberate unregulated economy cash. As it challenges the most holy of government syndications, Bitcoin shifts the pendulum of power away from states for people, offering us the enticing chance of a reality where cash is completely removed from legislative issues and excessive by borders.

The last section of the book investigates probably the most well-known questions encompassing Bitcoin: Is Bitcoin mining a hopeless cause? Is Bitcoin for crooks? Who controls Bitcoin, and might they at any point change it assuming they please? How might Bitcoin be killed? Also, what to think about every one of the a large number of

Bitcoin knockoffs, and the many guessed utilizations of Bitcoin's 'block chain innovation'? The Bitcoin Standard is the fundamental asset for an unmistakable comprehension of the ascent of the Internet's decentralized, objective, unregulated economy option in contrast to public national banks.

Chapter 2

What is Bitcoin great for?

Bitcoin is only a virtual money or a mode of managing computerized exchanges, very much like some other advanced cash. So what improve it than our traditional money?

Recently, the worldwide interest in bitcoins has developed. Thus, it turns out to be critical to grasp the foundation of this and any remaining types of virtual monetary standards. Bitcoin, and its options are totally founded on cryptographic calculations which are encoded. This makes the money decentralized giving possession to the user.These can be bought through an internet based trade or a Bitcoin ATM. Milestone element of a bitcoin is that it can check the possibilities of extortion and character robberies, and subsequently is viewed as a protected method of holding money.Bitcoins permit purchasing of labor and products on the web, as well as moving cash.

The following are a couple of advantages of utilizing bitcoins which improve it than any customary money:

Bitcoin is advanced and decentralized - With Bitcoin individuals get the freedom to trade esteem without mediators which mean more noteworthy control of assets and lower charges. It's quicker, less expensive, safer and unchanging. Cash is constrained by banks while bitcoin has proprietors.

Simplicity of web based shopping: As we definitely know, Bitcoin can assist us with doing internet shopping.

It resembles an e-wallet which can be made blockchain innovation to store, track and spend advanced cash.

Less unstable than cash: Bitcoin has a worldwide acknowledgment and is less unpredictable than cash/nearby money. Because of this component, it becomes simpler to go through with exchanges across limits and on the web.

No genuine approach to monitoring customary money The basic innovation behind bitcoin, which is, blockchain represents the moment of truth it. Large number of PCs in a disseminated network utilize cryptographic strategies to make a long-lasting, freely available report of each and every Bitcoin exchange that has at any point happened. This record will be truly important for different things other than following installment. While there is no genuine approach to following money.

Extraordinary instrument for speculation Bitcoin can be utilized all around the world without going through a change interaction. It is considered at standard with Gold and consolidates the best of money and gold while giving an open market and no limitations forced by banks or states.

Bitcoin is shared and open, yet secure and almost frictionless - Bitcoin permits trading esteem over the web with practically no mediator and gives its clients admittance to their equilibrium through a secret word known as a confidential key. So it's private, secure and at the equivalent time,open.

Duplication inconceivable - There is not a chance of copying a bitcoin, in contrast to cash.

Incredible approach to keeping up with records for charge purposes: Once moved, a bitcoins' possession likewise gets moved. This implies that two individuals can't be executing on a similar worth and this will assist with keeping records solid and less complex, particularly for charge purposes.

Transnational computerized money - There are no limits to

Bitcoin or digital currency. No trade values and no outsider intercessions. Bitcoin permits consistent exchanges across countries with a record getting kept up with at the backend

Chapter 3

Is Bitcoin a safe store of value?

By Mark Jeftovic

robert hunt (1923) german hyperinflation just posted this in the thread, Do you think Bitcoin is a safe store of value? on the Corner of Berkshire and Fairfax (some of the smartest value investors you've never heard of frequent that board, it's one of my favorite investing boards on the internet) and it occurred to me that it may have come across somewhat vitriolic and rant-ish for such a serious forum and it probably was more suited to a stand-alone post here:

It is not possible to fully grasp the ramifications of bitcoin until one reads The Onion's

"U.S. Economy Grinds To Halt As Nation Realizes Money Just A Symbolic, Mutually Shared Illusion"

...realizes the truth behind what makes it so funny, and goes on to realize that the underlying insight behind it is more fully applicable to the US Dollar than it is to bitcoin.

At that point, you will realize that crypto currencies are a true game-changer and that the price action of bitcoin is but a mere side-show.

Money evolves over time, who can deny that? And it usually evolved along lines of expediency and in a counter-trend to government policy (which is always in one direction: inflate and debase). Today the official national currencies are again being systematically destroyed by their governments, and this is happening across all currencies simultaneously. Given the needs of a global, interconnected, highly abstract economy facing these circumstances, crypto-currencies were pretty well inevitable.

Yes, new crypto-currencies can emerge (there already are hundreds of them and most of them are dying on the vine – the most comical one I've come across is zimcoin, which actually claims to be pegged to the Zimbabwe dollar at the rate of $10 trillion $Z to one zimcoin)

The important thing about this is it puts currency itself back where it should be: subject to market forces. Thus, if one currency elects to destroy itself via mismanagement or dilution (a.k.a inflation), the market participants can and will move out of it. This is as it should be.

Fiat currencies like all national currencies are currently engaged in a worldwide game of dirty pool. We're in a global currency war, there is open talk of ZIRP becoming NIRP, governments and central banks are basically screwing everyone in an effort to keep an unsustainable paradigm going.

Nearly every single criticism I've seen leveled against bitcoin is more accurately applied against the US dollar, or the Canadian dollar, or the Euro or the Yen. You want to talk about "meaningless numbers in a computer somewhere?" look no further than those currencies. You want to talk Ponzi? Look at QE, Abenomics and other "wealth effect" gimmicks that enrich those closest to the politically connected and screw everybody outside the beltway.

That "the government will eventually shut bitcoin down"

is also easy to deflect: they can’t. Shutting down bitcoin would be about the same as banning prime numbers. Sure they may go after exchange providers, maybe they drive it completely underground, but then they just create it as a black and grey market. Further, to make a real go of “shutting down bitcoin” it will require a push into global totalitarianism that makes today’s situation (with it’s global surveillance and the suspension of most civil rights) look tame.

The reason for all this is because pretty well every global government, and their complicit central banks, especially in the US, especially in the UK, especially in Canada, especially in Europe, everywhere, with their desperate economic rigging and central planning, with their pervasive global surveillance on their own subjects, with one illegal war, police action, "peace keeping", bail-in, bail-out and nationalization after another have lost all legitimacy to rule.

So the emergence of something like bitcoin, necessity being the mother of invention, was just one big F.U from the free market to the system that it's been holding its head underwater for decades. It had to come out somewhere, here it is.

Crypto-currencies are inelastic forms of exchange, which put them in the same league as gold or silver, and no, they will never replace them, rather they have emerged as a perfect compliment to them. Totally portable, frictionless and largely immune to capital controls, crypto-currencies have become the official lubricant of the free market (I mean the real free market, the one where price discovery actually takes place between buyers and sellers, not dictated by central planners).

This isn't a curiosity, this isn't tulipmania, and no, I'm not recommending you run out and buy bitcoin (it'll probably crash down to about $100 or $200 any time now, maybe lower) – but I would recommend setting up a bitcoin wallet somewhere, getting an exchange account and obtaining the ability to move funds in and out of it as needed so you are comfortable doing so.

If you own a business, start accepting bitcoin. I've been accepting it since spring of this year, so that's how I've accumulated all of mine. Sure, it's nice to be nominally "up" on the exchange rate, but that isn't why I'm doing it. I've sold a bit of it just to familiarize myself with the ins-and-outs of converting to cash, and I have a debit card which I can load up with bitcoin and withdraw dollars from any standard ATM.

End rant.

Chapter 4

Savings are for Suckers

Canute bans bitcoin. The grotesque side-effects of years upon years of ZIRP are beginning to peek out from under the proverbial carpet that policy makers and apologists have continually swept them.

The easiest way to think of present-day monetary policy is as a coordinated centrally planned effort to suspend consequences by edict in a profound King Canute episode of economic folly.

As we've explored before, when interest rates are artificially suppressed, all money becomes "hot money" as it has to chase yield anywhere it can get it. (When the music finally stops I predict a forthcoming crisis particularly in seniors who have been hounded out of meagre fixed income returns and into "safe equities that will never go down because the Fed won't it happen").

So given the data points:

- ➢ Cyprus, which was serially restructured through a

process of Calvinball economics to make a depositor bail-in retroactively "legal".

- Those "bail-in" provisions quickly hopped the Atlantic and found it's way into Canadian budgetary policy.
- The IMF floats various "one-time" haircuts simultaneously across all depositors. (ZeroHedge: IMF Discusses "One-Off" Wealth Tax")

And banks are now acting on their own:

- JPM Chase recently enacted a policy to limit business account wire transfers destined for foreign accounts to $50,000 per cycle. (ZeroHedge: Creeping Capital Controls at JPM Chase)
- Now (too big to prosecute) HSBC limiting cash withdrawals of their own customers' deposits "unless they can provide evidence to why they want it". (BBC: HSBC Imposes Restrictions on Large Cash Withdrawals)

It gets worse.

Negative interest rates are no longer unthinkable monetary policy absurdities that should make everybody realize how horrifically unstable the global financial system has become by mere virtue of having a trial balloon floated.

Janet Yellen who pined for them last year is now Chairman of the Fed. She was in ostensibly stiff competition for the position with Larry Summers, who also spoke up in favor of them.

Mario Draghi speaks of negative interest rates as a distinct possibility.

So….

Given that:

- We face a future where negative interest rates are not unthinkable, they may very well be likely.
- Banks are now arbitrarily implementing capital controls on their own customers
- Not to mention that instead of depositing money in banks and earning 0.5% interest you

could simply buy their preferred shares and capture a 5% coupon (although I would be wary of that, just sayin')

Why on earth would anybody actually deposit money in a bank?

Will it be any surprise then, when old-school savers start squirreling their money under the mattress, but that still won't put their wealth out of reach of confiscatory governments since they are officially targeting higher inflation (Globe and Mail: Bank of Canada's Poloz ponders lack of inflation).

When the realization sinks in, that's when a genuine buying panic into physical gold and silver starts.

So can anybody really be surprised at all at the ascent of Bitcoin?

bankster_govner_bitcoin

One of the fallacies of those downplaying the significance of Bitcoin is that there is "no official government backing" of it as a form of money or currency.

This demonstrates ignorance of monetary history as anybody who cares to look will discover that when something takes on monetary functions it happens outside of governments. Then over time, the paper representations of a commodity-backed money (the fiduciary medium) becomes inexorably co-opted through government malfeasance and fractional reserve banking until the medium is no longer backed by anything.

It plays out over such a long period of time that the general public fails to notice that a profound change has occurred in their monetary system.

Detlev S. Schlichter's Paper Money Collapse gives a good overview of this process by which a useful commodity becomes imbued with monetary properties, acquires exchange value apart from its use value and begins to be used as a medium of exchange.

Until now this has played out with commodity backed money, but henceforth will be complimented by cryptographically secured currencies, such as Bitcoin.

What they have in common is that they are both inelastic forms of money, which is anathema to governments and central bankers. Their sentiment could best be summed up in their chief apologist Paul Krugman, who opined, quite simply “Bitcoin is Evil”.

Tell a pensioner, who’s been eking out a living on a fixed-income in a mult-year ZIRP environment that NIRP is coming, that within the next few years he should factor on perhaps 25% to 50% of his savings to be confiscated in some sort of co-ordinated bail-in to rescue his bankrupt government, and until that happens that same government will be trying it's damnedest to ignite inflation and when he decides to pull what little he has left out of the bank to sock under his mattress, have the bank tell him "Uhm, no sorry, we can't let you do that".

Then tell him that deflation (and ergo Bitcoin) is evil – because it can't be inflated by government decree, because it becomes more valuable and can buy more over time, because it cannot be confiscated or be subject to capital controls, and what will he say?

Perhaps he will quote Machiavelli:

"...there will be traits considered good that, if followed, will lead to ruin, while other traits, considered vices which if practiced achieve security and well being.

Chapter 5

Imminent Death of Bitcoin Predicted

By Mark Jeftovic

Hundred (100) bitcoin will buy this car. I have noticed Business Insider's Henry Blodget's typically frantic sensationalism which trumpets "news" such as his "Bitcoin could go to $1 million", where he goes on to attempt to take down the currency as something that is in a bubble and will eventually become worthless:

"But I was getting at a more profound point. $400 is a perfectly reasonable target for Bitcoin. As is $1,000. As is $10,000 or $100,000 or $1 million. And as is $0.01.

In his writings, Blodget seems on a mission to deconstruct bitcoin, dismiss it as a bubble and a fad.

However, as I am now growing tired of observing, nearly every single criticism I see levelled at bitcoin is more appropriately applicable to fiat currency.

Among Blodget's favourite arguments is that Bitcoin "has no value" because:

"Unlike gold or dollars or other things that have widely accepted utility, Bitcoin's price is determined entirely by what someone else is willing to pay for it."

It's true that I don't have a degree in economics and no central banking experience, but I'm not exactly financially illiterate and I'm at a loss to think of any good, commodity or service exchanged in an ostensibly free market whose value is not ”determined entirely” by what somebody else willing to pay for it. Unless you count things where the value is also determined by what some counter-party is simultaneously willing to sell it for, but in any case, this still includes bitcoin, and everything else in the known universe of free markets.

There is no “inherent price” in anything, there is only what market participants are willing to pay for things. The only exceptions are government edicts like currency pegs and price controls and everybody knows, none of that stuff works. In command economies price discovery tends to occur in burgeoning black and grey markets and guess what? Those too set prices based purely on what people are willing to buy and sell at. This is not news, at least it shouldn't be.

In a another article Blodget flogs the point:

"There is absolutely no way to value Bitcoin, which means there is nothing constraining its price other than supply and demand."

Again, what's Blodget's point? This isn't some incontrovertible damning of Bitcoin, it's a vapid truism.

I'm not saying that the bitcoin price will continue its meteoric ascent (in fact if I were a day trader I'd be betting against it)

But I will comment (again) that even ifsomething's price action is really in a bubble – that doesn't mean that it is worthless and will go to zero after the price action blows off, or that the underlying phenomenon loses all utility after a crash. In fact that is more the exception than the norm.

But what I will say is bitcoin specifically and crypto currencies in general are here to stay. This is the evolution of money.

The criticisms levelled against bitcoin and crypto-currencies in general are rife with profound misunderstanding, gross irony or just plain raw, defensive fear. Blodget prides himself on having written extensively on bitcoin, let's look at a couple of his arguments:

It will never be widely accepted because:

1) governments will ban it or

2) it's too complicated and "shadowy"

These are easy, #1 – they can't. A government "banning bitcoin" is akin to a government banning prime numbers. They may pass the edict, it won't really change much. Any full-on banning of the use of bitcoin in private transactions will only further bankrupt the government of any remaining credibility and further alienate the political class from the real world.

Number 2, that bitcoin is “too complicated and shadowy” is a pretty solid argument and difficult to refute. A good example of this is how the internet never gained any traction and pretty well died in the crib around 1994 because it was overly complicated and shadowy.

Blodget is probably right about the price action of Bitcoin being in a bubble, or at least headed for one. It’s certainly in a secular bull market now, and as Henry says, it could be a long time and a lot higher before it blows off. But the price action of bitcoin is a sideshow. In the overall scheme of things, crypto-currencies are here to stay and that is where all the real action is. It isn't about buying a few bitcoin now and making a pile of money off it later. This is short-sighted.

What it's really about is providing lubricant for capital flight when the next government tries to recapitalize it's zombie banks out of its subjects savings. It's about unhindered mobility of capital. It's about complete transactional privacy. It's about providing basic functions of money and currency that the current powers-that-be have mishandled and lost all credibility for handling. It's an inelastic currency and that makes it sound money and it's the perfect compliment to gold and silver.

To paraphrase Amschel Rothschild, who famously opined:

"Give me control of a nation's money and I care not who makes it's laws"

I counter with:

"Give me a crypto-currency and I care not who abuses their power"

www.ingramcontent.com/pod-product-compliance
Lightning Source LLC
LaVergne TN
LVHW050348160826
845677LV00014B/3847

* 9 7 9 8 8 4 7 7 9 3 1 4 8 *